THE FUNNIEST SUNDERLAND QUOTES... EVER!

Also available

The Funniest Liverpool Quotes... Ever!

The Funniest Chelsea Quotes... Ever!

The Funniest West Ham Quotes... Ever!

The Funniest Spurs Quotes... Ever!

The Funniest Arsenal Quotes... Ever!

The Funniest Man City Quotes... Ever!

The Funniest Newcastle Quotes... Ever!

The Funniest United Quotes... Ever!

The Funniest Celtic Quotes... Ever!

The Funniest QPR Quotes... Ever!

The Funniest Everton Quotes... Ever!

The Funniest Rangers Quotes... Ever!

Mad All Over: The Funniest Crystal Palace Quotes... Ever!

Fergie Time: The Funniest Sir Alex Ferguson Quotes... Ever!

I Am The Normal One: The Funniest Jurgen Klopp Quotes... Ever!

I Didn't See It: The Funniest Arsene Wenger Quotes... Ever!

Zlatan Style: The Funniest Zlatan Ibrahimovic Quotes!

'Arry: The Funniest Harry Redknapp Quotes!

War of Words: The Funniest Neil Warnock Quotes!

Chuffed as a Badger: The Funniest Ian Holloway Quotes!

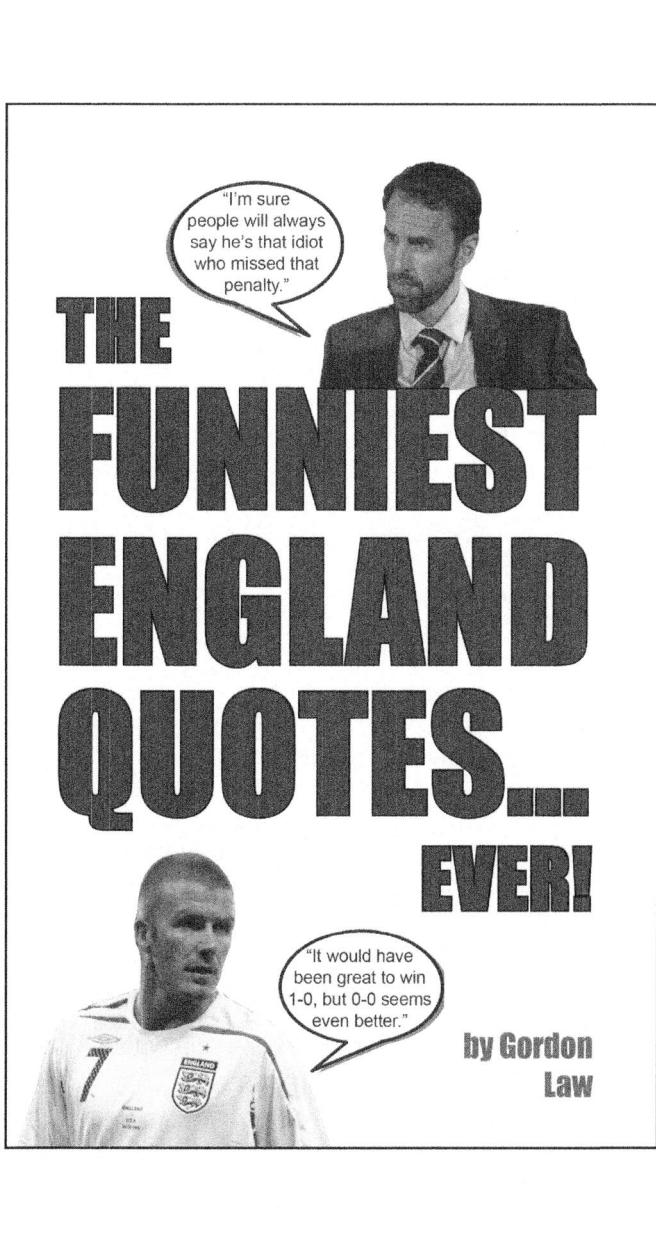

"I'm sure people will always say he's that idiot who missed that penalty."

THE FUNNIEST ENGLAND QUOTES... EVER!

"It would have been great to win 1-0, but 0-0 seems even better."

by Gordon Law

Copyright © 2020 by Gordon Law

No part of this publication may be reproduced, stored in a retrieval system or transmitted in any form by any means, electronic, mechanical, photocopying, or otherwise, without prior written permission of the publisher Gordon Law.

gordonlawauthor@yahoo.com

Printed in Europe and the USA
ISBN: 9798694167246
Imprint: Independently published

Photos courtesy of: Influential Photography/Shutterstock.com; Joel Orme/Shutterstock.com

Contents

Introduction..6

Calling The Shots..9

Field Of Dreams..19

Talking Balls..33

Boardroom Banter...41

Can You Manage?...47

Off The Pitch...57

Managing Just Fine.......................................67

Game For a Laugh..79

Media Circus...87

Pundit Paradise...93

Fan Fever..101

Introduction

Sunderland has provided its supporters with plenty of drama over the years – especially with the number of colourful personalities that have spent time at the club.

During dark moments on the field, there's been some amusing, inspirational and downright daft comments that have raised a chuckle off it too.

Manager Roy Keane is a journalist's dream for providing entertaining quotes and his blistering tirades at players or critical take on the state of modern football are always fascinating to hear.

When he's not turning the air blue, Keane can show his humorous side with a sarcastic quip to a reporter and even have the humility to take the mickey out of himself.

Straight-talking Mick McCarthy's brutal honesty and quick wit made him another compelling character to have been in charge at the Stadium of Light.

Paolo Di Canio came out with some bonkers remarks, there were many strange musings from Howard Wilkinson, while Steve Bruce's banter produced plenty of laughs.

There's been ace anecdotes from Danny Higginbotham, pearls of wisdom from Jason McAteer and humdingers from Anton Ferdinand.

Many more rants and foot-in-mouth moments can be found in this unique collection of funny Sunderland quotes and I hope you laugh as much reading this book as I did in compiling it.

Gordon Law

THE FUNNIEST SUNDERLAND QUOTES... EVER!

CALLING THE SHOTS

"[Anthony] Stokes could be a top, top player in four or five years or he could be playing non-league."
Roy Keane

"It was Milan and Prada or Sunderland and Primark."
Steve Bruce on hoping to beat AC Milan for David Beckham's signature

"Craig's not going to Barbados – we've got a nice seafront down here. As long as he doesn't go out in a canoe we'll be all right."
Roy Keane tells Craig Gordon he's not going abroad

"We have to help with the travel arrangements. If we left it to them (the Trinidad & Tobago FA), I think he'd be on a ferry."

Roy Keane on getting Kenwyne Jones back from his game in the Caribbean

"Those two players [Lee Cattermole and Phil Bardsley] were rotten. The most unprofessional players I ever worked with."

Paolo Di Canio blasts the duo after his exit

"It's not really the same. He's from Dublin, you see. Dubliners are different – like cockneys."

Roy Keane when asked if Anthony Stokes resembled a younger version of himself

THE FUNNIEST SUNDERLAND QUOTES... EVER!

"On a night we got beaten in the cup by Luton, the staff came in and said, 'Clive Clarke has had a heart attack at Leicester'. I said, 'Is he OK? I'm shocked they found one, you could never tell by the way he plays'. Clarke later goes and does a piece in some newspaper telling the world that I have lost the dressing room. How does he know? He wasn't there! Clown."

Roy Keane on his Sunderland defender, out on loan with Leicester

"No disrespect to the country. It's a wonderful place, the... Where's he gone again?"

Steve Bruce after Asamoah Gyan's move to the United Arab Emirates

Calling The Shots

"I got Robbie's [Savage] mobile number and rang him. It went to his voicemail: 'Hi, it's Robbie – whazzup!' Like the Budweiser ad. I never called him back. I thought, 'I can't be f*cking signing that'."

Roy Keane

"He said, 'Yesterday I had a food poisoning'. Sorry, are you the doctor?"

Paolo Di Canio blasts an unnamed player for not having a doctor's note

"A few days after I left Sunderland, Yorkie text me, 'All the best'. I text him back, 'Go f*ck yourself'."

Roy Keane on Dwight Yorke

THE FUNNIEST SUNDERLAND QUOTES... EVER!

"The other day in training, he wanted to join in an 11-a-side game and I had to say to him, 'Kyler, no!'. And he went away and kicked three or four balls all over the pitch. Then he was made to go and fetch them because he had thrown his toys out of the pram."

Mick McCarthy on the injured Kevin Kyle

"[John O'Shea] should say sorry to some of his teammates for the many times he came into my office to say something unfavourable about them. The same person that also came to me when I first took over and said things about [Martin] O'Neill."

Paolo Di Canio fires shots after his exit

Calling The Shots

"Like I keep telling people, he's 18 years of age, 18! Jesus, what were you doing when you were 18? The things I was doing at 18? Disgraceful!"
Roy Keane on Anthony Stokes

"If you are driving to work, don't get into a car with Liam Miller because he gets involved in more car crashes than anybody I know."
Roy Keane after he transfer-listed Liam Miller for repeatedly being late for training

"Keeping Jonny Evans long term? There is probably more chance of England's cricketers winning the World Cup."
Roy Keane on trying to sign the United star

THE FUNNIEST SUNDERLAND QUOTES... EVER!

"You're the reason I'm driving up and down the f*cking country to find another player, you're not f*cking good enough... Your attitude is sh*t. And you're not good enough..."

Roy Keane blasts individual players after a defeat during the 2007/08 season, recounts Danny Higginbotham

"You know at the end of the season when you walk around the pitch, thank the fans for their support? I'm ringing Umbro and getting you some hooded jumpers, because you're a f*cking embarrassment. It's a joke and this is not going to stay this way."

Roy Keane continues his tirade

Calling The Shots

"Kelvin lost his voice and couldn't call for the ball in the last 20 minutes. At first I dismissed it because it sounds like bullsh*t, but it's a stonewall genuine problem."
Mick McCarthy on keeper Kelvin Davis

"I knew Andy was a good player. I had to carry him in a few games for Ireland, but I knew he had a chance... he's not six foot four, I don't think he ever will be."
Roy Keane on Andy Reid

"I did invite him to Take That, but he declined."
Steve Bruce still trying to lure David Beckham to Sunderland

THE FUNNIEST SUNDERLAND QUOTES... EVER!

FIELD OF DREAMS

"If they have more desire and play less empty in the brain, they can keep the ball much better. At this moment, they are empty. John O'Shea did something that was unacceptable at this level."
Paolo Di Canio after defeat at Palace

"When you've got ears like mine you don't miss anything the crowd chants."
Peter Reid on abuse from Sunderland fans

"It wasn't a monkey on my back, it was Planet of the Apes!"
Mick McCarthy after a win over Middlesbrough gave his team a rare league win

Field Of Dreams

"I don't want to start swearing like Joe Kinnear, but to say I was slightly aggrieved would be a posh way of putting it."
Roy Keane on Sunderland's disallowed goal against Fulham

"It was going to be my first 1-0 win that I was going to celebrate with my family on Mothers' Day tomorrow, and it would have been unbelievable. But now I'm going to be crying into my wine, I'll tell you that now. I'm not going to be very happy and sadly I hope I don't take it out on my grandkids, but I'll try not to."
Sam Allardyce rues two dropped points against Southampton

THE FUNNIEST SUNDERLAND QUOTES... EVER!

"You shouldn't be collecting players' autographs."
Roy Keane after his side suffer a club record 10th consecutive Premier League away loss

"I didn't realise I was liked by so many people here. It was a lovely term of endearment, wasn't it?"
Mick McCarthy after Millwall fans chanted abuse at their former manager

"I started clapping myself, until I realised that I was Sunderland's manager."
Peter Reid after Dennis Bergkamp scored a fine goal for Arsenal

Field Of Dreams

"The last song before the players went on to the pitch was Dancing Queen by Abba. What really worried me was that none of the players – not one – said, 'Get that sh*t off'. They were going out to play a match, men versus men, testosterone levels were high. You've got to hit people at pace. F*cking Dancing Queen. It worried me. I didn't have as many leaders as I thought."
Roy Keane

"The biggest problem we had was that we conceded three own goals in the first half."
Howard Wilkinson after a 3-1 defeat to Charlton

THE FUNNIEST SUNDERLAND QUOTES... EVER!

"A blundering full back could've stuck a couple of those in – from about four leagues below."
Martin O'Neill on the wasted chances in a 1-0 loss to Chelsea

"This win means I may be able to leave the house now."
Roy Keane after a triumph over Derby

"Upset? No, I would have joined them if I could."
Mick McCarthy on the thousands of fans who left the Stadium of Light early during Sunderland's 4-1 defeat by Portsmouth

Field Of Dreams

Sunderland fan: "How do you feel?"

Chris Coleman: "I feel responsible."

Fan: "You haven't got a f*cking clue, mate."

Coleman: "OK. You don't know me very well."

Fan: "B*llshit. F*cking pr*ck."

Coleman: "You calling me a pr*ck? I'm a married man with six kids."

Chris Coleman is confronted by an angry supporter outside the ground after Sunderland are officially relegated

"I thought I'd have to throw another ball on the pitch for us to get a kick."

Bob Stokoe after Sunderland were outplayed by Man City but managed to nick a draw

THE FUNNIEST SUNDERLAND QUOTES... EVER!

"I'll celebrate with a green tea and a chocolate biscuit."

Roy Keane after Sunderland beat Spurs

"I was talking to Claudio Ranieri after the game and he said he thought they were playing Real Madrid in the first half."

Mick McCarthy enjoys his chat with the Chelsea manager

"Our biggest mistake was turning up."

Ricky Sbragia on Sunderland's defeat to West Brom

Field Of Dreams

"I think his haircut helps. Having my hair cut used to help me. I used to feel leaner and sharper. Meaner. So I might shave mine next month."
Roy Keane after Craig Gordon's heroics against Wigan

"Giving a penalty to someone else because you feel sorry for him, because he has not scored, is the sort of thing you do in the school playground, not the Premier League."
Steve Bruce on usual penalty taker Darren Bent handing the duty to his teammate Kenwyne Jones

THE FUNNIEST SUNDERLAND QUOTES... EVER!

"I haven't got enough time to tell you – Match of the Day only lasts an hour and 20 minutes, doesn't it?"

Mick McCarthy when asked what went wrong after Sunderland's loss to Villa

"We weren't beaten today, we lost."

Howard Wilkinson

"He's quick upstairs, that's what matters. Like he showed for the goal today, my instructions for him were to sit, so he's obviously listened to me and bombed forward and scored a goal."

Roy Keane on Dwight Yorke

Field Of Dreams

"Me walk away? What? Never. I always believe that I am the best manager in the world. Why should I have to walk out? I have been working 24 hours a day. The players have to adapt to me, to one person. I cannot be a fake Di Canio."

Paolo Di Canio before his final game, a 3-0 defeat against West Brom

"I still believe in myself. I will never change. The players need to release the rubbish from their brains."

Paolo Di Canio continues after the Baggies loss. He was sacked the next day

THE FUNNIEST SUNDERLAND QUOTES... EVER!

"Mr Wenger is a very clever man, but I have to say that what he said was cr*p."

Peter Reid after Sunderland's encounter with Arsenal

"Before the goal it was two rubbish teams playing rubbish football."

Mick McCarthy on the 1-0 defeat against Birmingham

"I have never witnessed anything like that, not at this level anyway – maybe when I was at school."

Steve Bruce after defeat to Blackpool

Field Of Dreams

"My magic words at half-time were f*ck, b*llocks, b*stard, cr*p and p*ss-poor."
Mick McCarthy on the game at QPR

"That's f*cking sh*te! And it's not about f*cking tactics and them being f*cking great players, it's about f*cking a*sehole – they've got more on the f*cking day. So f*cking get on with it!"
Peter Reid's half-time tirade against Wimbledon

"I was excited and it takes a lot to get me excited – ask my wife."
Roy Keane after a win over Spurs

THE FUNNIEST SUNDERLAND QUOTES... EVER!

TALKING BALLS

"My mum wasn't too pleased as it was the first Christmas I had missed."

James McClean on playing through the festive period

"That's the second time I've been sent off for celebrating. I'm going to staple my shirt on in the future."

Ross Wallace

"Everyone was scared of him... He's got a temper. Like in training, if things aren't going his way, he'll boot all the balls out the drill."

Lewis Morgan on Aiden McGeady

Talking Balls

"The [tactics] board goes up. And Keano takes a running jump and smashes it over with a kung fu kick. He screamed at Danny Collins, 'Never come and ask me for a contract again'. And then the captain, Dean Whitehead, is next. 'Captain? Captain? Some f*cking captain you'."
Dwight Yorke on Roy Keane

"He scared me half to death. You didn't want to be on the end of one of his bollockings. The first thing he ever said to me was, 'You may have heard that I'm a b*stard... Well, they're right'. And yes, he could be. But he was a brilliant one."
Brian Clough on manager Alan Brown

THE FUNNIEST SUNDERLAND QUOTES... EVER!

"My grandma was there and after the game she said, 'Have you seen all these French flags? They are for you'. It was funny because she didn't realise they were not for me, but for Eric [Cantona]."

Lionel Perez after a 5-0 defeat against Manchester United

"Paolo went mad when he first saw the players' buffet, full of grease. He shouted in his funny English with a heavy Italian accent, 'What is this? What is this? Is this a wedding?' It was hilarious."

Simon Mignolet on Paolo Di Canio

Talking Balls

"He didn't say much, we were introduced to him briefly and he shook hands with everyone. I'll be honest, I was a bit frightened myself."
Daryl Murphy on Roy Keane

"The season before I was the best thing since sliced bread."
James McClean

"The boss doesn't talk to me, he doesn't even say hello when he sees me. I think he doesn't like me because I'm not English. Steve Bruce is not a nice person at all. He is a little unpleasant."
Marcos Angeleri

"He said, 'Listen lads. Basically, you're sh*t. Try and enjoy the game. You're probably going to get beat. But just enjoy being sh*t'. Then he just walked out."

Danny Higginbotham on a Roy Keane team talk

"As a player, he was a ranter and a raver. But I think he's taken it back a bit. He's just a ranter now."

Paul McShane on Roy Keane

"I am special, just like I am on the pitch."

El Hadji Diouf

"John Byrne says his hair is natural. He must be using natural bleach."

Paul Bracewell

"I not only did my knee, I banged my head. A lot of people have put it down to the way I've behaved for the last 10 years."

Brian Clough on his career-ending knee injury at Sunderland

"Nobody is interested in my England caps, in me finishing seventh in the Premier League with Sunderland or Blackburn... All they want to hear about is that bloody penalty."

Michael Gray on the promotion-winning kick

THE FUNNIEST SUNDERLAND QUOTES... EVER!

BOARDROOM BANTER

THE FUNNIEST SUNDERLAND QUOTES... EVER!

"If a Russian billionaire came in I would not only roll out the red carpet but I would hoist up the red flag."
Bob Murray

"If any one ugly b*stard was going to beat us, I'm glad it was you!"
Niall Quinn to Mick McCarthy after a Wolves victory

"I can't afford to pay for the pizzas we've ordered now!"
Stewart Donald after shelling out £3million for Will Grigg on transfer deadline day

Boardroom Banter

"If it all goes well it is worth it, if not... well, it's better one day a lion, than 30 years a pussycat."
Niall Quinn on his boardroom role

"I've given them [the Sunderland board] the list of the three or four players I want. I know they can't arrive until January, but it's a bit like Christmas – I'm hoping that when I come down the stairs they'll be under the tree."
Roy Keane

"The p*ss-take party stops now."
Charlie Methven doesn't want agents milking the club

"I'm loving working with Mick. I find Mick very South Yorkshire, very honest indeed. He's very... I wouldn't say black and white, I would say red and white. There doesn't seem to be a bit of pink in the middle. If it's Friday today, it's Friday. He's slow to get his [drinks] round in, but I'm really enjoying working with him."
Bob Murray on Mick McCarthy

"He spoke to me like I was something on the bottom of his shoe... It's probably true that the relationship was never going to work, and not because he was some big, bad Texan and I was some grumpy Northsider from Cork. I don't like being spoken down to."
Roy Keane on Ellis Short

Boardroom Banter

"The local pubs aren't happy that there's 25,000 and not 48,000 in the ground. And then there's the nearby strip club and the strippers aren't too happy either. It's bad for top totty and the lap-dancing club has closed."
Bob Murray on Sunderland's relegation

"It is like being in a goldfish bowl, as it was when I was a player. As a chairman it's like that, except someone has stuck a blender in there as well. And switched it on."
Niall Quinn

"It is a failed, f*cked-up business – 100% f*cked."
Charlie Methven on joining the club

THE FUNNIEST SUNDERLAND QUOTES... EVER!

CAN YOU MANAGE?

"I'm aware as a manager I cannot go off the handle as much as I did, but if I feel something is not right I will look to nail it – just with a bit more subtlety."

Roy Keane

"I like wingers who veer, but I prefer them to veer straight."

Billy Elliott

"The players have to adapt to me. I am a warrior."

Paolo Di Canio

Can You Manage?

"It irritates me a little. These sort of awards always did, even when I was a player, so I'll have to say it'll probably go in the garage."
Roy Keane is not overjoyed to receive his Manager of the Month prize

"As one door closes, another one shuts."
Howard Wilkinson

"It's amazing when you do apologise – it's a relief to both sides. Will I apologise to Mick McCarthy? We'll see."
Roy Keane after saying sorry to Niall Quinn

"The other lads will be asking Jason McAteer, 'What's he like? Is he all right? Has he got a sense of humour? What's his training and coaching like? Is he is a big-nosed miserable sod?"

Mick McCarthy on his arrival at the club. He managed McAteer as Ireland boss

"I had no interest in going straight into management. My plan was to chill out for a few years and spend time with my family, but they got fed up with me. It was a family decision. The wife dropped me off here."

Roy Keane

Can You Manage?

"As a player you could physically go up against people. As a manager it is not really allowed!"
Roy Keane

"I'm going to be on a learning curve and it's one I'm looking forward to. People go on about my inexperience, but one or two managers with experience have not worked out at Sunderland."
Roy Keane – referring to Mick McCarthy?

"Yee-ha! I've looked like I've had a coat hanger in my mouth ever since."
Mick McCarthy on being appointed manager

"I don't think I'll ever be happy – it's not in my nature or in my blood. I get glimpses of it. If we go up I might allow myself a smile for 10 seconds."

Roy Keane

"Some say my ego is as big as an elephant. They're wrong. It's 10,000 times bigger than that. As big as the world."

Paolo Di Canio shortly before joining Sunderland

"You can't give a team confidence. You can't put it in a pill, or a suppository."

Howard Wilkinson

Can You Manage?

"I had a leather chair that swung around, a swivel chair. For the first few days I used to swing around on it. If any of the players or the staff had peeped through the office window they would have seen me going, 'Weeehhhh!'"
Roy Keane

Q: "Would you experiment with the Christmas tree formation?"
Steve Bruce: "I'm not really into tactics."

Journalist: "Great players don't always make great managers."
Roy Keane: "That's all right because I was never a great player."

"If people are worried about me losing my temper in certain situations, trust me, they've seen nothing yet. If people are worried now, by Jesus."

Roy Keane

"As a manager, it's your head on the block. You have to make cold-blooded decisions and if you can't, you shouldn't be in the job. To be honest, I found it difficult to be a b*stard."

Terry Butcher

"There's certainly no uncertainty about my future."

Roy Keane before stepping down

Can You Manage?

"I know the Romans came 2,000 years ago. They conquered the North East and were here for 100 years. Maybe after two months it will be, 'Di Canio f*ck off, bye bye Paolo'. It can happen but I'm sure it won't."
Paolo Di Canio on arriving at Sunderland

Q: "Will you be staying on after May?"
Dick Advocaat: "With Sunderland? No, no, no. I get a divorce!"

"If they wanted the players smiling all the time they should have employed Roy Chubby Brown rather than me."
Roy Keane after departing Sunderland

THE FUNNIEST SUNDERLAND QUOTES... EVER!

OFF THE PITCH

"It's not about going out with your friend and getting back at two or three in the morning, which is late. You can close one eye. But not full of alcohol and walking like this."

Paolo Di Canio after Phil Bardsley was seen on a casino floor surrounded by £50 notes

"Always I give a second chance to the people. He is not a kid, he has a family at home. I'm not here to be a priest."

Di Canio continues on Bardsley

"There's a word you don't hear around footballers' dressing rooms any more – mortgage."

Niall Quinn

Off The Pitch

"I did a 24-hour sponsored silence for Children In Need and if I hadn't had my girlfriend to talk to, I think I would have struggled."
Anton Ferdinand

"I took my wife out on Saturday night but all I was thinking about was our back four. It was like taking the back four out as well."
Roy Keane

Q: "What's more satisfying, scoring a hat-trick or having great sex?"
A: "The missus might be reading this, so I'd better say the sex."
Kevin Phillips

THE FUNNIEST SUNDERLAND QUOTES... EVER!

"From now on, if someone comes inside with a mobile phone, even in their bag, I'll throw it in the North Sea. They're banned."

Paolo Di Canio

"My Lyon teammates told me I spoke French like a Spanish cow."

Mick McCarthy

"Before, when the players said, 'I've been out and drunk seven beers', the masseurs participated. They wouldn't say, 'It's not good. It's wrong'."

Paolo Di Canio

Off The Pitch

"I have to walk. If I couldn't I'd be in a padded cell by now."
Roy Keane on how he manages to relax

"He's stopped putting things in his throat, basically. It's quite simple."
Steve Bruce on Andy Reid's dietary plan

"It was like moving from Butlin's to Belsen."
Brian Clough on relocating from Middlesbrough to Sunderland

"I'm North East born and bred now."
Liverpudlian Len Ashurst

"I do transcendental meditation and I have done it for 12 years now, ever since I was introduced to the person who took me through the ritual process. It's very relaxing, very calming and you can do it anywhere. It helps you cope with the pressure you come under in this job."

Sam Allardyce

"I was asked to see one in France and I came out of it with my arm around him consoling him."

Mick McCarthy on his meeting with a sports psychologist

"If they don't want to come [to Sunderland] because their wife wants to go shopping in London, it's a sad state of affairs. To me, that player is weak because his wife runs his life."

Roy Keane on missing out on players as their partners wanted to go shopping in the capital

"There's a fine line between loyalty and madness and I'm not sure which side he's on. I think it's madness."

Gary Rowell after a supporter changed his name to 'Gary Sunderland AFC Lamb' and said Rowell was his favourite player

THE FUNNIEST SUNDERLAND QUOTES... EVER!

"I started on Shrove Tuesday and then by Ash Wednesday something had happened and I'd had a bottle of beer."

Mick McCarthy on giving up booze for Lent

"We need to have lectures about why we can't have things like mayonnaise, ketchup and Coke every day."

Paolo Di Canio

"I suppose getting the sack gives you the chance to do it."

Steve Bruce on watching the England cricket team play Pakistan in Dubai

Off The Pitch

"I won't be watching the Newcastle-Boro game, I will be tearing my hair out in the pub."

Ricky Sbragia

"If Donald Trump wants to come and see the boys, he's very welcome. Maybe we'll go to Trump Tower."

David Moyes on a New York team bonding jaunt

"I know many players who had ice with Coke the night before games. It causes congestion and they can't play properly."

Paolo Di Canio

THE FUNNIEST SUNDERLAND QUOTES... EVER!

MANAGING JUST FINE

THE FUNNIEST SUNDERLAND QUOTES... EVER!

"Paolo Di Canio? That managerial charlatan? Paolo stepped in there and basically, as weeks ran on, he ran out of excuses. I had a wry smile to myself."

Martin O'Neill on the Italian's stint as boss

"A charlatan is a manager who spends £40m to be a top-10 club and then sees the club sink into the relegation zone."

Paolo Di Canio after Martin O'Neill had labelled him "a managerial charlatan"

"Some chief executives are trying to take our pants down."

Steve Bruce on his transfer woes

Managing Just Fine

"You can only bring in kids from a certain radius and a lot of our radius is in the water. Any good fish out there?"

Roy Keane

"At the moment, I know where we are. We're bottom of the table."

Howard Wilkinson

"Yes, I'd be interested in the Ireland job. It would have to be in a few years' time – and they'd all have to go, the whole of the FAI, every single blazer and committee man. But can you imagine me working for the FAI?"

Roy Keane

THE FUNNIEST SUNDERLAND QUOTES... EVER!

"We have to believe we can get something on Sunday. In a two-horse race, you have to believe. Arsenal might get stuck on the Tube."
Roy Keane

"Jose Mourinho has some of the best players in the world at Chelsea but we are not going to roll over on our bellies, get tickled, and say, 'Isn't it great we're in the Premiership?'"
Mick McCarthy

"Our squad looks good on paper, but paper teams win paper cups."
Howard Wilkinson

Managing Just Fine

"Of course they were on time. More than on time. They were so early they brought the milk in."

Roy Keane after he dropped three players for being late for the bus

"To be honest, I have never been part of a group of players that went to the chairman, because that is for cowards."

Paolo Di Canio on his time at Sunderland

"Niall [Quinn] was interviewed after the game... He looked about a hundred."

Roy Keane before he took manager's job

THE FUNNIEST SUNDERLAND QUOTES... EVER!

"The man's a clown. He sent me a letter and he was quite happy to give it to the media. I spoke to him and told him what I thought about him and where I think he should go. He is writing these letters and it is always under the FIFA heading just to impress everybody. If he is vice president of FIFA then God help us. People worry about the game and agents and directors of football and managers losing their jobs – we should be worried about people like him."

Roy Keane on FIFA vice president Jack Warner after he ordered Dwight Yorke back from international duty with Trinidad & Tobago

Managing Just Fine

"It is easier to play Chelsea or Manchester City in the Premiership than Cheltenham at home."
Mick McCarthy

"I'm not expecting hugs and kisses... there won't be a red carpet rolled out for me."
Roy Keane ahead of locking horns with his old coach Carlos Queiroz

"A lucky goal or the run of the ball can be triggers, but they can only be triggers if you have gunpowder."
Howard Wilkinson

THE FUNNIEST SUNDERLAND QUOTES... EVER!

"I always thought that they were an arrogant bunch, for a club that had won f*ck all. We always got decent results at St James' Park; it wasn't a bad place to play. But as for the Toon Army, the Geordies and the hostile reception – I never fell for all that cr*p."

Roy Keane on Newcastle

"We all know that in football, you stand still if you go backwards."

Peter Reid

"Too often we've been on the losing end of a defeat."

Roy Keane

Managing Just Fine

"I don't think the rumours have affected my players. When I reported to meet the team, I think they were more disappointed than anyone I hadn't resigned."

Roy Keane on suggestions he had departed the club

"Like trying to turn around an oil tanker with a canoe paddle."

Mick McCarthy on Chris Coleman's chances as Sunderland manager

"If you don't score at this level, unfortunately you aren't going to get a win."

Steve Bruce

THE FUNNIEST SUNDERLAND QUOTES... EVER!

"The last time I was charged by the FA they had a murder lawyer in against me, so it's going to be a hard case to win."

Roy Keane on an FA misconduct charge

"In the relegation zone it's three from four because, in my mind, we're already out of it."

Howard Wilkinson

"Every single one of the players has been slapped around the head but they still keep coming back for more."

Mick McCarthy after they beat West Brom in only their second league win of the season

Managing Just Fine

"You call me the mad Italian so I will bet all I've got."

Paolo Di Canio is backing Sunderland to stay up

"The game at Reading, just before Christmas, was the only time I really lost my temper as a manager. I'd lost my temper before – but I'd used my temper. This time I used physical force. I grabbed a staff member, put his head on a table, and tried to pull his tie off. But he was a Reading staff member, not one of ours..."

Roy Keane on clashing with Reading's Kevin Dillon

THE FUNNIEST SUNDERLAND QUOTES... EVER!

GAME FOR A LAUGH

"It was a horrible, horrible debut... I was devastated... it was a long weekend for me. I couldn't even say I could take the dog out for a walk because I haven't got a dog."
Andy Cole after a 7-1 defeat at Everton

"The atmosphere in the dressing room was toxic, we would have lots of fights."
Jan Kirchhoff's fond memories of the club

"I'm not too sure how it will work out. I actually thought of putting a glove in my sock to pull out if I score."
Anton Ferdinand on paying his respects to Michael Jackson if he scores

"It may be a problem getting a few players to move up here, but I'm originally from Lapland so I don't really mind where I live. It's the one question that always seems to come up when I speak to journalists, 'How's Lapland? What's Santa Claus like?' Don't get me wrong, it's nice to talk about home but when it's every time, it gets boring. I'm like, 'What about the football?'."

Finland international Teemu Tainio

"I do not want to talk about my contract, but many things will be easier if Sunderland drop down."

Jeremain Lens, on loan at Fenerbahce, hopes Sunderland get relegated

"Who would refuse Lyon? Me, I would go there on foot to sign. For the moment, they haven't called me. But I do not hide the fact that I am happy a big club is interested in me."

Pascal Chimbonda is clearly fully committed to Sunderland

"Win bonus? What's that? Do we get them? We had one once. Hopefully we will get a little bit of something now."

Liam Lawrence

"I got one or two goals a season, give or take the odd 30."

Brian Clough on his goalscoring feats

"This club is very much like an Ireland team – we drink a lot and run around like nutters."
Jason McAteer welcomes Mick McCarthy

"If you are in a house that catches fire and you are running around, screaming and shouting, if you are panicking, the children will start crying and you will all be burnt."
Christian Bassila says the team must remain calm during a bad run of form

"We had a bit of Abba on before a game this season. It might explain the kind of start we had!"
Graham Kavanagh

THE FUNNIEST SUNDERLAND QUOTES... EVER!

"I don't give a damn about the record. Kylie Minogue makes records."

Jason McAteer on Sunderland's losing run

"I'll keep going and hopefully push Charlton. Charlton? Sunderland up the league."

Darren Bent forgets which team he plays for after his beach-ball goal

"I'm delighted to be a Sunderland player and it's an honour to join this club."

Younes Kaboul after his agent Rudy Raba had previously said: "Younes would not join Sunderland – even if there was an earthquake."

Game For a Laugh

"I'm just as good as Peter Schmeichel, but I'm more modest by nature."
Thomas Sorensen

"Can you tweet something like unbelievable support yesterday and great effort by the lads! Hard result to take! But we go again!"
Victor Anichebe makes a Twitter faux pas

"Dennis Wise has made a living out of being a cheat... Dennis tries to be your mate all the time but he quickly forgets that he's just kicked you in the head, two-footed you or stuck his finger in your ear."
Jason McAteer

THE FUNNIEST SUNDERLAND QUOTES... EVER!

MEDIA CIRCUS

"It was getting a wee bit naughty at the end there so just watch yourself. You still might get a slap even though you're a woman. Careful the next time you come in."

David Moyes to the BBC's Vicki Sparks after he was unhappy with her questions

"The problem is you, not me. I'm not going to get involved any more. If we close Sunderland – if we put a China Wall around the city – it would be fantastic. Now when we let you in and you get out and say what you want we've got a problem. I invite every Sunderland fan and people around the club not to listen to any one of you – only to me."

Gus Poyet to reporters

Media Circus

Q: "After the England v Germany game, you said you wouldn't like to be the next Premiership manager to face Michael Owen. Now you must feel pretty much the same about David Beckham?"

Peter Reid: "Hmm, well, David isn't playing today."

Exchange on Sky Sports before Sunderland's match with Man United

"Will those on telly yesterday be remembered for what they've achieved? None whatsoever. I wouldn't trust them to walk my dog. There are ex-players and ex-referees being given air-time who I wouldn't listen to in a pub."

Roy Keane on the TV pundits

THE FUNNIEST SUNDERLAND QUOTES... EVER!

"If we go down, I'll hide somewhere in the middle of Asia. If we stay up, you will see me in every single newspaper on a beach somewhere famous."
Gus Poyet

"Am I scared? No! And neither should you be!"
Mick McCarthy tells reporters that he's confident Sunderland will stay up

"What other way would you approach a game? Must-lose? Must-draw?"
Roy Keane when asked if it was a "must-win game"

Media Circus

"Jesus Christ, if I start losing sleep over Phil Babb I'm in trouble. Babbsie is prone to coming up with all sorts of stuff. He is paid by Sky."

Roy Keane on being told Phil Babb fuelled rumours that he had left Sunderland

Reporter: "Are you aware of the rules regarding an outside agent like the beach ball?"

Steve Bruce: "You have to be pretty sad if you know that rule and I believe you know it don't you. You must be the only one in 55,000 people here today."

After Darren Bent's shot went in the net off a beach ball on the pitch against Liverpool

THE FUNNIEST SUNDERLAND QUOTES... EVER!

PUNDIT PARADISE

THE FUNNIEST SUNDERLAND QUOTES... EVER!

"Late goals come in short bursts and Sunderland's burst has gone on for a long time."

Phil Thompson

Q: "Do you think Roy Keane will make a good manager one day?"

A: "No, I don't think so."

Niall Quinn in 2005, a year before he appointed Keane as Black Cats boss

"Sunderland are breathing down the shorts of Wigan."

Mark Bright

"Paolo Di Canio managed with a bar of iron."

Paul Merson

"Sunderland have edged this one by a long, long way for me."

Kevin Keegan

"Tense and nervous aren't the words, Jeff, but they are, if you know what I mean..."

Chris Kamara during a Sunderland-Hull meeting

"Sunderland could rub salt in Newcastle's faces."

Graham Courtney

THE FUNNIEST SUNDERLAND QUOTES... EVER!

"They'd better take away his bootlaces, his belt and his tie after that."

Mark Lawrenson feels for Mick McCarthy after a defeat to Birmingham

"Prica has scored for Sunderland – his dad is rumoured to be called Pap."

Ian Payne

"If Mick McCarthy can get a result with that midfield – Proctor, Williams, Thornton and Gray – he is a miracle worker."

Chris Kamara

Pundit Paradise

"He's one of the biggest whingers in world football. He's a bloody eejit."

Eamon Dunphy on Mick McCarthy

"Sunderland played tremendously well for 90 minutes, but they didn't play very well for the first 15 minutes."

Lee Dixon

"I think Everton [to win], but if Sunderland won this game... It would really throw the pigeons among the cats."

Paul Merson

THE FUNNIEST SUNDERLAND QUOTES... EVER!

"Sunderland have started like a house on fire!"

Chris Kamara

"Dwight Yorke has come off – and the only man who could replace him... was the son of a Prica man."

Jeff Stelling on substitute Rade Prica

"Backsides and opinions, we've all got them. But it's not always a good idea to air them in public."

Mick McCarthy after Roy Keane departed Sunderland

Pundit Paradise

"I always think Newcastle v Sunderland is very much a tale of two cities."
Colin Cooper

"Both sides' supporters are singing the same chant – 'There's only one Keano' – which makes them both wrong, to be honest."
Match of the Day commentator during the Sunderland-Spurs game

"It's never over until it's over, but this is over."
Chris Kamara on Sunderland v Bolton

THE FUNNIEST SUNDERLAND QUOTES... EVER!

FAN FEVER

THE FUNNIEST SUNDERLAND QUOTES... EVER!

"Sunderland's gone down and we couldn't give a f*ck. Cos we got, Aiden McGeady. We'll win the league and we'll go straight back up. Cos we got, Aiden McGeady."

An ode to the midfielder, sung to Whigfield's Saturday Night

"He's our keeper, our Belgian keeper, he's Simon Mignolet."

The fans' version of In The Jungle

"They tried to get the ball past Nyron, he said no, no, no."

Nosworthy's song, to the melody of Amy Winehouse's Rehab

Fan Fever

"Steed Malbranque, Malbranque. He plays on the left or right. He makes your defence look sh*te. Steed Malbranque, Malbranque."

To the tune of Doris Day's Whatever Will Be

"God took Messi and Pele. Mixed the two to make one. And he came up with, Stephane Sessegnon."

The fans put the midfielder in esteemed company

"It's Jozy Altidore. You know he's gonna score. We'll go wild wild wild. We'll go wild wild wild."

The striker's chant to the tune of Slade's Cum On Feel the Noize

THE FUNNIEST SUNDERLAND QUOTES... EVER!

"Who's gonna get past Michael Turner? Who's gonna get past Michael Turner? No one can get past him. Turner, up he rises. Turner, up he rises. Turner, up he rises. Scoring goals from corners!"

Honouring Michael Turner, the fans' version of What Shall We Do With The Drunken Sailor

"And here's to you, Mrs Advocaat. Wearside loves you more than you will know. Woah!"

Sung to the melody of the Paul Simon hit Mrs Robinson

"Who needs Mourinho? We've got Roy Kean-eo!"

The fans celebrate the manager

Fan Fever

"Niall Quinn's taxi cabs are the best, so shove it up your a*se, Easyjet. Fat Freddie wouldn't do it for the Mags. Niall Quinn's taxi cabs!"

Sung by supporters after Quinn spent £8,000 on taxis for stranded fans

"You've been hit by, you've been struck by... Lee Cattermole."

An adapted version of Michael Jackson's Smooth Criminal

"Andy Reid, he plays left wing. He loves McDonald's and Burger King."

The midfielder's chant, to the tune of The Piranhas' Tom Hark

"Oh Lorik Cana. There's no one harder. He came from Marseille. To Wearside. He's our captain. And quite outstandin'. Please don't take our Lorik away."

Sung to the tune of You Are My Sunshine

"Your chicken is dead. Your chicken is dead. Kevin Nolan, your chicken is dead."

Poking fun at Kevin Nolan for his chicken celebration

"His name's not Rio and he plays for Sunderland. He came with McCartney, his name's Anton Ferdinand."

The defender's version of Duran Duran's Rio

Fan Fever

"He's big, he's thick, he's got a ginger d*ck. Paul McShane, Paul McShane."

A unique chant for the Irishman

"He loves his flashy underwear, Cisse, Cisse. He's got designer facial, Cisse, Cisse. He scores a goal with half a chance, we'll never send him back to France. Djibril Cisse. Sunderland's number nine."

The fans honour the striker

"Sulley Muntari's having a party, bring your vodka and Bacardi!"

The supporters go wild when he scores

THE FUNNIEST SUNDERLAND QUOTES... EVER!

Printed in Great Britain
by Amazon